Animal Show-offs

Written by Nancy O'Connor

Flying Start
to Literacy®

Contents

Introduction

Sometimes, animals show off. They use loud sounds or make themselves look big and strong. Some animals show off by decorating the places where they live.

Animals show off for different reasons. Some animals show off to protect the places where they live. Other animals show off to find a mate, and some show off to scare away other animals.

4

Chapter 1:
Get out!

Sometimes animals want to keep other animals out of their territory. They show off in many different ways so other animals stay out of their territory.

Lions

A lion's roar is one of the loudest sounds on Earth. When a lion roars, it is letting other animals know to stay away from its territory. A lion roars to show that it is fierce and strong.

Sounding out
When a lion roars at night, its roar can be heard as far as 8 kilometres away.

Giraffes

Giraffes are gentle animals. But giraffes will fight if a new giraffe wanders into their territory.

Fights begin with lots of pushing and shoving, which looks like showing off. Then the giraffes slam their heads and necks into each other.

What a weapon

A giraffe's neck is about 2 metres long and weighs over 220 kilograms. When the giraffe swings its neck, it is like using a heavy club.

8

Giraffes also use their short horns to try to
injure each other. The winner of the fight
keeps the territory.

Meerkats

Meerkats live together in large family groups called mobs. But even though they are small, meerkats can make themselves look big and scary.

The mob bands together to fight off another mob that tries to take over their territory. They fluff up their fur to make themselves look bigger. Then they jump and bark loudly to show how big and strong they are to scare away the other mob.

Chapter 2:
Finding a mate

Many animals show themselves off to find a mate.

Bowerbirds

Male bowerbirds show off their building skills. They do this to get the attention of female bowerbirds. They use grass and sticks to build a shelter called a bower.

Male bowerbirds also like to decorate their bowers. When the males have finished decorating, female bowerbirds hop from bower to bower. They choose the one they like the best.

Home beautiful

Bowerbirds put stones, berries, feathers, seashells and flowers in front of their bowers to decorate them.

13

Elk

Male elk fight each other to win the attention of female elk.

Every autumn, the teenage male elk get together to show off by fighting. They raise their heads and make loud screaming sounds, called bugling. This behaviour shows they are looking for another elk to fight.

Amazing antlers
An elk's antlers can grow up to 1.5 metres long.

When an elk finds another elk to fight, the animals crash their antlers together and they get tangled.

When one elk gives up and runs away, the winner looks around to see which female is watching.

Pufferfish

Pufferfish are small fish that live in the sea. Male pufferfish make huge circle patterns in the sand on the bottom of the sea to find a mate.

Male pufferfish swim back and forth and move the sand with their fins to make the patterns. It can take a week for a fish to finish his circle pattern.

Sand circles

Pufferfish are only about 12 centimetres long, but the circles they make can be 2 metres in diameter.

Then female pufferfish swim by to see which pattern they like best.

Chapter 3:
Danger warning

Some animals show off to protect themselves from other animals. They scare other animals away.

Elephants

Elephants are the biggest animals that live on land. They don't feel threatened often. When an elephant does feel threatened, it flaps its ears, raises its head high and swishes its trunk.

Sometimes, angry elephants throw dust and break tree branches with their trunks to look scary.

Walk the walk
Elephants can walk backwards and forwards, but cannot trot, run or gallop.

Hippopotamuses

When a hippopotamus yawns, watch out! It is showing off its enormous teeth and trying to scare away other animals.

Hippos have long teeth that are very dangerous. Some of their teeth are more than 30 centimetres long.

When a hippo feels threatened, it will attack. A hippopotamus may look large and heavy, but it can run faster than a human.

Huge hippos

Hippos can grow up to 4.5 metres in length and weigh almost 2,000 kilograms. That is as big as a car!

Conclusion

Animals have many different ways of getting attention by showing off.

Protecting their territory

Showing off	Animal	
Roars	Lion	
Fights	Giraffe	
Makes itself look big and scary	Meerkat	

Finding a mate

Showing off	Animal	
Builds and decorates a bower	Bowerbird	
Bugles Fights	Elk	
Designs circle patterns	Pufferfish	

Danger warning

Showing off	Animal	
Flaps ears and swishes trunk	Elephant	
Shows off teeth Runs fast	Hippo	

Index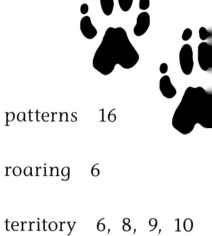

24